INDIAN SCULPTURE IN THE JOHN AND MABLE RINGLING MUSEUM OF ART

by Roy C. Craven, Jr.

University of Florida Monographs
HUMANITIES
No. 6, Winter 1961

UNIVERSITY OF FLORIDA PRESS / GAINESVILLE, FLORIDA

EDITORIAL COMMITTEE

Humanities Monographs

T. WALTER HERBERT, *Chairman*
Professor of English

CLINTON ADAMS
Professor of Art

CHARLES W. MORRIS
Professor of Philosophy

C. A. ROBERTSON
Professor of English

MELVIN E. VALK
Associate Professor of German

COPYRIGHT, 1961, BY THE BOARD OF
COMMISSIONERS OF STATE INSTITUTIONS OF FLORIDA

LIBRARY OF CONGRESS
CATALOGUE CARD No. 61-63517

PRINTED BY THE BULKLEY-NEWMAN PRINTING COMPANY
TALLAHASSEE, FLORIDA

PREFACE

In 1956 a group of Indian sculptures was placed on display in the loggia of the John and Mable Ringling Museum of Art. These seventeen works were purchased by Mr. John Ringling in the thirties at the close of his collecting career, and then lay hidden in the museum's basement for some thirty years. Records which could tell of how and where these sculptures were obtained have been lost, but the fact that they constitute a rich gift to the people of Florida is apparent in the works themselves. Today they become even more significant as interest in America quickens for the great cultures of the Orient.

The present study undertakes to describe fourteen of these sculptures (Three minor pieces, Plates 15, 16, and 17, are not discussed in the body of the text, but are reproduced and identified in the Plate section.) in such fashion as to provide each with its date, with its region of origin, and with an explanatory description of its religious or mythological subject matter. I have presented the sculptures in chronological sequence without attempting to provide extensive historical data. This the reader may find in standard histories of Indian art. It is hoped that the accompanying map and the chronological table will be illuminating.

Many people have earned my gratitude for their help on this project; here I must mention Professors Allen Sievers and John Spencer, who read and commented on the manuscript; Mr. Don Denny, Dr. Barbara Ebersole, Mrs. Helen Haines of the University of Florida Press, and Professor Walter Herbert of the University of Florida Humanities Monograph Committee for correcting and working out many technical aspects; Professor W. Norman Brown for identifying and translating the inscription on the image in Plate 10; Mr. Charles O'Neal for his assistance in photographing the works at the museum; Professor F. Van Deren Coke for the photograph which became Plate 12A; and as always Lorna Craven for her untiring help and encouragement.

The generous permission of individuals, publishers, and museums to quote and to reproduce photographs from their works is hereby acknowledged: Mrs. A. K. Coomaraswamy of Cambridge, Massachusetts, Figures C and E; Dr. I. Grafe of the Phaidon Press, London, figures D and M; Mr. George Hill of Bruno Cassirer, Ltd., London, Figures J and K; Mr. B. L. Mankad, Director of the Baroda Museum and Picture Gallery, Figure L; Mr. V. P. Mathur of the Archaeological Museum, Mathurā, Figure B; Miss Joan Rassieur of the Museum of Fine Arts, Boston, Figure I; D. H. Sahiar, *Marg* Magazine, Bombay, Figures G and H; Mr. S. P. Srivastava, Director of Archaeology and Museums, Rājasthan, Jaipur, Figures J and K; Mr. V. S. Srivastv, Curator of the Ganga Golden Jubilee Museum, Bikānēr; Mr. A. H. N. Vermey, Rijksmuseum voor Volkenkunde, Leiden, Figure F; and Mr. Archibald Gibson Wenley, Director of the Freer Gallery of Art, Washington, Figure A. The plates are reproduced from photographs taken by the author at the Ringling Museum in Sarasota, Florida.

I would especially like to cite Mr. Kenneth Donahue, Director of the John and Mable Ringling Museum of Art, who brought these Indian sculptures out of their darkened exile and once again presented them to an appreciative public.

ROY C. CRAVEN, JR.

GAINESVILLE, FLORIDA
NOVEMBER, 1960

CONTENTS

Preface	iii
Map of the Subcontinent of India	vi
Text	1
Plates and Figures *follow page*	14
Chronological Table	25
Bibliography	27

Map I. The subcontinent of India showing sites mentioned in text.

The most significant achievement in Indian art was that of the sculptors.[1] Working in remote antiquity, they created a robust record of one of the world's oldest continuous civilizations—a record which proves to be a revealing image of the aesthetic as well as the religious realities of the Indian mind.

Small sculptured pieces from the Indus Valley civilization, created during the second or third millennium B. C., displayed a highly developed skill and plastic awareness. These qualities are evident in the three-dimensional figures of stone and metal as well as in the many toy animals of clay recovered from the ruined cities. Some Middle-Eastern influence is apparent in the numerous intaglio seals, but the early florescence of the indigenous style, competent in craftsmanship and sensitive to aesthetic considerations, is truly Indian.

The cities of the Indus were destroyed around 1500 B. C. by the conquering Āryans who brought with them from the steppes of central Asia their rude nomadic culture. Thus a sophisticated and ordered civilization succumbed to a primitive and virile one. From this period up to the time of the Buddha few physical works remain, but literary sources tell how the Āryan import, blending with the indigenous cults and traditions, evolved into a new Indian culture.

Two great religions other than Vedic-Brāhmanism were to originate with this evolving culture. The Buddhist and Jain movements both developed from Brāhmanism as reforms, but where Jainism was a projection and refinement of the parent religion, Buddhism became a true schism with complete autonomy. Each sect originated with a historic savior: Gautama Siddhārtha (c. 563-483 B. C.) was the founder of Buddhism, while his contemporary, Mahāvīra (c. 540-468 B. C.), was the first *tirthankara* (teacher) of the Jains.

1. The word Indian or India in this paper refers to the whole geographical subcontinent, which today includes both countries of India and Pakistan.

The first great Buddhist king, Aśoka (c. 273-232 B. C.), zealously propagated the new faith throughout his vast empire, which stretched southward from the northern mountains and the area now known as Afghānistān across to all but the extreme tip of the Indian subcontinent. This flourishing state religion produced the first Buddhist works of art, but this early activity was only the beginning.

Figure A
By the second century B. C. the masterworks on the great railing at Bhārhut, in central India, had been carved (Figure A), and early in the following century the gates at Sānchī were created. Other works at Sānchī as well as the first reliefs at Amarāvatī were executed later, during the active period from the last century before Christ through the first century of the new era. The momentum thus gained was accelerated, and by the second and third centuries, Buddhists were engaged in tremendous artistic production throughout India.

The first Indian sculptures in the John and Mable Ringling Museum of Art actually date from this later period of the third century and come from the ancient and famous region known as Gandhāra. This area, located in what today is northern Pakistan and eastern Afghānistān, was invaded and conquered around A. D. 65 by a nomadic tribe known as the Yueh-Chih, who pushed into India and established the Kuṣāna empire. Under its patronage and the stimulus of Buddhism the region produced a distinct style of sculpture which was to influence subsequent schools of art not only in India but throughout Asia.

In this area and elsewhere in India, at the beginning of the Christian era, Buddhism underwent a transformation, and the older and more orthodox form of Buddhism known as "the lesser vehicle," or *Hinayāna*, was being challenged by a more humanistic concept. This new concept was later to be known as "the greater vehicle," or the *Mahāyāna* doctrine. With the advent of this movement the Buddha, in art, takes on a deified human form, and whereas in the past his holy presence had been symbolized as a tree, wheel, umbrella, footprints, and other nonhuman forms (Figure A), he now began to be delineated as an actual human savior.

Figure A

The origin and appearance of the human form of Buddha have been the subject of many scholarly investigations and still seem to elude the clear light of certainty. May scholars have felt that the Buddha figure was a Hellenic inspiration, entering Indian art in Gandhāra, while others assert that this realism was nothing new to the Indian scene, and that indigenous Buddhist sculptors had previously perfected a Buddha figure inspired by Indian prototypes.[2] We know that the Gandhāran area, for some time prior to the first century, had been in direct and extended contact with the West. Alexander the Great, in 326 B. C., had penetrated into India as far as Taxila, eventually one of the chief sites for Gandhāran sculpture, and from that time forward a more or less direct contact with the Mediterranean world existed. The Greek kingdoms of Bactria, northwest of Gandhāra, had lasted almost until the beginning of the first century B. C., and later, current with the Fourth Buddhist Council (c. A. D. 100, a time which also marks the approximate schism between the *Hinayāna* and *Mahāyāna* factions), an envoy was sent to Trajan in Rome. Other political and economic relations between East and West might be cited, but the most significant fact to be remembered is that by the second century itinerant Roman sculptors were probably at work in Gandhāra.[3] Therefore, it would seem that the Buddha figure is of an Indo-Roman origin and probably came into being in the Gandhāran area sometime around the beginning of the Christian era. But perhaps it is only necessary to know that the abstracted and symbolized deity became delineated into a recognizable human form after the religious climate had been altered by the more liberal doctrine of *Mahāyāna*.[4]

The first example from Gandhāra is an excellent piece and depicts the episode from the Buddha's life which occurred, according to legend, seven weeks after the enlightenment at the base of the Bo-tree (Plate 1). Returning from a journey, two merchants with five hundred chariots were passing near the holy tree when the wheels sank into the ground and refused to move. The merchants discovered the Holy One, paid him homage, and offered him food. Now the four *lokapālas*, or Guardians of the Quarters of Heaven, who had been watching from above, knew that the Buddha had no bowl with which to receive the alms, and immediately offered him bowls of gold. These the Buddha rejected as inappropriate for alms, as he did the ones of silver and of emeralds which followed. At last he accepted simple stone bowls, and with them he received

Plate 1

---

2. See Coomaraswamy, "Origin of the Buddha Figure," pp. 287-329.
3. Rowland, *Art and Architecture of India*, p. 73.
4. For a discussion of Mahāyāna Buddhism, see Zimmer, *Philosophies of India*, pp. 507-534.

the merchants' offerings. He blessed the merchants and they went their way rejoicing.

In the sculptural fragment the right half of the scene has been broken away, and only the maimed image of the seated Buddha and a procession of figures remain to the left. The fracture runs across the piece diagonally, cutting into the halo and head of the Buddha but leaving his body and low throne intact. Two *lokapālas*, holding bowls, lean in and give a thrust of action toward the central figure of the lord, while a third figure, possibly holding a flower blossom in his raised right hand, stands to the extreme left and closes off the scene. Above him two broken figures fade at their waists into the background and share the top region with a stylized tree. At the extreme left of the piece, two figures, one standing and one above fading into the background, are all that remain of another episode. Between them and the scene of the presentation of the bowls stands a vertical niche containing a column with an ornate Persepolitan capital composed of animals. This type of capital was known in India from the time of Aśoka, and its presence here further illustrates the cosmopolitan character of the Gandhāran sculptural style. The column unit is a typical device used by the sculptors of Gandhāra to divide the episodes of a sculptural narrative. The method of displaying the narrative of the Buddha's life in a continuous horizontal frieze made up of separate self-contained sculptural "pictures" was constantly used on Gandhāran buildings and stupas, and served as an unending visual sermon to the devotee. The convex face of this relief suggests that it may have originally formed a segment of a sculptural narrative circling a stupa.

This work displays some Western influence, but the main mood and underlying action is typically Indian and is reminiscent of earlier Buddhist works carved at Amarāvatī. This excellent Gandhāran piece must have been executed at some time during the first half of the third century.[5]

Plate 2

The next work is a small *bodhisattva* figure seated upon a simple throne backed by a large circular halo which rises from behind his shoulders (Plate 2). This Buddha-to-be is the *bodhisattva*

---

5. In dating the Gandhāran works many references were consulted, but most useful were the excellent text and plates found in the exhibition catalogue by Professor Rowland, *Gandhāra Sculpture from Pakistan Museums* and Marshall, *Buddhist Art of Gandhāra*.

Maitreya, or the Buddha who will next appear on earth, and is identified by the *amrta* jug which he holds in his left hand. Because of this *bodhisattva's* benevolent quality we can be sure that his broken right hand must have originally performed the *abhayamudrā*. This gesture of assurance and protection is made by raising the right hand with its palm facing outward and the fingers raised and joined. Other distinctive marks of identity are the *ūrnā*, or a tuft of hair shown as a small round dot above the bridge of the nose, and the *ushnisha*, which is the protuberance on the top of the head and shows here as a crown of hair. This elaborate treatment of the hair, a classical element, shows how strong the Roman influence was in Gandhāra. A stylized necklace hangs from the figure's neck, as does a pendant from his undamaged left ear, and a bracelet is seen on the left wrist. The robe twines over and around the left shoulder and arm leaving the right shoulder and the trunk bare. Mathurān influence is evidenced by the excessively large ringed halo and the two exposed feet.[6] The low throne is supported at each corner by legs fashioned after those of a lion. Heavy, compact, and precisely carved, this sculpture at first seems removed from the mainstreams of the Gandhāran style, but in reality these qualities are the mannerisms of "the melancholy process of decline" and are generally found in the works of the "later maturity period."[7] Therefore a date of the last half of the third century is suggested for this unique work.

The museum's next piece from Gandhāra presents another architectural relief (Plate 3). Two compositional arrangements are contained within the vertical structure of the stone, and they suggest that the piece was originally part of a door jamb or some similar architectural feature.

Plate 3

It is interesting to contrast this work with the first example, the presentation of the begging bowls, and to see the "frozen" feeling here in this third piece. It is not as finished or as competent as the

---

6. Mathurā, modern Muttra, located thirty miles north of Agra on the Jumna River, has been a religious center from ancient times. It has been important to the Jains, Buddhists, and Hindus, and is associated with the birth and life of Śrī Krishna. An early seat of Jain art activity, a fact which some scholars feel points to an Indian origin of the Buddha image, Mathurā later produced a distinctive style of Buddhist sculpture. This style was contemporary with the art of Gandhāra and Amarāvatī and influenced not only current and subsequent Buddhist and Hindu art, but that of the Jains as well.

7. See Marshall, *Buddhist Art of Gandhāra*, p. 103.

earlier work, and evident is a heavy and stiff cast to the style. The two scenes ares episodes from the Buddha's life, but exactly which two is difficult to say. Below, the Buddha is seen displaying the *abhāya-mudrā* to a variety of listeners. The figure at the Buddha's right shoulder with the circular headdress is the god Indra while at the Buddha's left shoulder Vajrapāni (see below) and the god Brahmā are seen. A woman standing to the Buddha's right and a monk to his left, whose face is broken away, seem to be holding similar objects. The objects which they carry are obscure, but since the woman is not dressed in royal attire and seems to wear a *sāri* over her head in the style of the common people, this scene might depict the episode where a casteless girl was accepted into the order. Buddha's favorite disciple, Ānanda, insisted that the girl, Prakriti, give him a drink of water. This she did despite caste regulations, which so pleased the Buddha that he made her a nun. Since a monk is the other chief figure in the composition this identification seems plausible.

The situation in the scene above is even more intriguing. The Buddha is again shown holding his hand in the "fear-not" or blessing *mudrā* and is surrounded by people of various types. Notice especially the seminude youth posed to the Buddha's left, who easily could have stepped from a Roman work of the first century, and who, since he carries a thunderbolt in his left hand, is identified as Vajrapāni, the constant companion of the Buddha in Gandhāran sculpture. Of more interest is the damaged and bearded figure standing to the Buddha's right. His threatening attitude and his demonic appearance, even to the suggested horns on the head, are items which tempt us to believe that we see here a *yaksha* (tutelary god) accosting the lord. This figure could indicate the episode where the Buddha defied and converted Atavika, the forest *yaksha*, who fed upon human flesh. The tree behind the *yaksha* figure further implies the subject.

Whatever the subjects of this stone may be, the interrupted architrave which permits a higher Buddha figure to dominate the groups, the fold patterns on the Buddha figures, and the widow's peak in the hairline of the Buddha again indicate a date of the third century.

A small fragment from the base of a standing Buddha or *bodhisattva* figure is of interest because the museum's records state that it was found in the Malakand Pass by the Chitral expedition in 1895 (Plate 6). All that remains of the large figure above is the front half of the right foot showing all five toes. Since the *bodhisattvas* generally are shown wearing sandals and the Buddha figures barefooted, and since there is no thong showing here between the toes, the evidence suggests that the missing figure was that of the Buddha. Beneath the foot is a floral frieze which is supported from below by a square pilaster surmounted by a Corinthian-like capital. This style of western capital with its flat pilaster is quite prevalent in Gandhāran sculpture after the first century, and is another tangible example of Hellenic influence. To the right of the pilaster are two figures facing toward the position where either a seated Buddha or a symbol would be located if that portion were not broken away. Judging by the width of the large foot, two other figures and a pilaster would complete that area of the missing pedestal. The small worshipful figures appear to be a man and a woman and are summarily carved and completely distorted, having the strange height ratio of four heads. This fragment also can be attributed to the third century.

Plate 6

The last Gandhāran relief comes, according to museum records, from Hoti-Mardan, and is unfortunately only a small remnant of a larger work (Plate 4). Prominently displaying paired parallel lines of drapery, it must date from the late third or early fourth century. This beautiful fragment with five figures in attitudes of adoration originally formed the left hand side of a larger work depicting the Buddha's first sermon. The three standing devotees are dressed in the garb of nobility, and the one to the extreme right wears a royal turban-like headdress similar to the ones we have observed on the figures in the museum's first example. Below, two monks are seated upon *gadis*, or platforms, decorated with geometric patterns. At the extreme right a partial image of a tree with stylized foliage closes off the unit.

Plate 4

Evident here is a sureness of execution and an elegant grace which, with the exception of the relief depicting the presentation of the begging bowls, is missing in most of the museum's other examples from Gandhāra. One wishes that fate might have spared this work's fragmentation because in this small masterpiece is seen an accomplishment which demanded more from the sculptor than did many larger works.

The Ringling Museum's next four sculptures are the products of the other religious movement which, like Buddhism, resulted from a reform of Brāhmanism. The religion of the *jinas* (victors), Jainism originated with Mahāvirā (great hero), who was born about 540 B. C. and was a contemporary of the Buddha.

Jainism, a religion of extreme austerity, sees all the universe as a living order of *jivas*, or souls. Not only do plants and animals have souls, but rocks, water, air, everything. The life of a Jain monk is governed by five vows: to abjure killing, stealing, lying, sexual activity, and the possessing of property. With the whole universe alive with souls, and any killing or other act of violence looked upon as the greatest of sins, the Jains have carried the concept of *ahimsā* (nonviolence to living things) to the greatest extremes. A devout monk will wear a veil over his mouth, not only to avoid breathing in the most minute living beings in the air, but to keep from overly harming the air itself as he breathes it! He also may carry a small broom with which to clear his path of ants and other insects that might be crushed as he walks along.[8]

The Jains do not consider Mahāvirā as the founder of their religion, but as the last of twenty-four great *tirthankaras* (makers-of-the-river-crossing), or teachers, who show the way to salvation. These teachers are shown in art as saints perfectly detached from earthly bondage, who through penance and abstention have not only cleansed themselves of their egos, but have purified their biological physiques as well. Originally the Jain monks rejected clothing and caste marks as symbols of involvement with the world, and went abroad completely naked. Some of the standing images of the *tirthankaras* are shown in the attitude known as *kāyotsarga*, or "dismissing the body." These icons of ideal purity present a series of saint images completely devoid of costume and physical aberration, which, because of this anonymous perfection, makes individual identity difficult. It is fortunate that each *tirthankara* is associated with a particular symbol or emblem (*lānchhana*) which is incorporated into works of art and served as the only clue to the identity of the image.

Plate 5

It is unfortunate that the museum's first Jain image, a *tirthankara* (Plate 5) is broken to the extent that no identifying symbol remains. But the figure, executed of red sandstone and seated in

8. For a discussion of Jainism see Zimmer, *Philosophies of India*, pp. 181-279.

dhyāna-mudrā (meditation) upon a lion throne, possesses a majestic serenity which is still impressive. Its head and hands have been broken away, and except for the complete nudity of the figure and the presence of the diamond shaped *śrīvatsa* jewel in the center of the broad and powerful chest, this image might easily be mistaken for a Buddha figure. It is this very close identity between the Jain and Buddhist images at Mathurā that previously suggested an exclusively Indian origin for the Buddha figure and tended to invalidate the theory of its creation by the Westernized art of Gandhāra.[9]

In the fragmentary background the headless body of a male attendant, or *yaksa*, stands to the left of the saint.[10] Originally he held a *cauri* (fly-whisk) in his missing right hand (see Plate 8). Plate 8 The lower legs and feet are all that remains of a similar figure to the saint's right. Beneath the *tīrthankara*, a *simhasāna* (lion-throne) displays a formal arrangement divided by a triangular shape which hangs down from the center of the seat. A drape and tassel hang at the top of this shape, and below them, seated in a worshipful attitude, two figures represent the donors of the image. Beneath the donors a series of fractures have removed the lower areas of the throne, and possibly with them has gone the saint's identifying symbol (again see Plate 8). To either side of the triangular shape Plate 8 a bejeweled lion is seen in a threatening attitude. With paws raised, eyes bulging, and tongues extended, the lions present a marked contrast to the composed and pacific figure of the saint. The lions, however, are symbolic of the saint's kingly and superhuman state, and their ferocity refers to his complete dedication to the victory over the illusions of worldly reality.[11]

---

9. Coomaraswamy, "Origin of the Buddha Figure," pp. 287-329.

10. "*Yaksas*, no less than *nāgas*, must have been very popular in the pre-Aryan tradition, to judge from the frequency of their occurrence both on early Buddhist monuments and in later Indian art. Dwelling in the hills and mountains, they are guardians of the precious metals, stones, and jewels in the womb of the earth, and so are bestowers of riches and prosperity. Two *yaksas* commonly are represented standing at either side of doors, carved on doorposts, as the guardians of the welfare of the home, and, according to Buddhist literary sources, a common feature in the inner yard of the ancient Hindu household was the standing figure of a gigantic *yaksa* as the tutelary god of the house."—Zimmer, *Art of Indian Asia*, I, 43-44.

11. "Such a throne is the common seat and symbol of regal dignity in the secular realm, where the king is lion among men. Comparably, the Enlightened One is the lion among spiritual teachers, philosophers, and divines, and when he lifts his voice to announce the doctrine every other voice is

Two figures seated at the corners of the throne are recessed from the plane of the lions and triangular shape. The one to the right appears to be a female and possibly displays the cobra hood of a *nāginī*, while the other seems to be a dwarf. The significance of both of these figures is obscure.

Even in its broken state the well-known style, iconography, and distinct red sandstone material of this image allow us to identify it as a fourth or fifth century figure of a Jain *tīrthankara* from Mathurā.[12]

Plate 8 The next image (Plate 8) is of a later date and, though considerably weathered, is more iconographically complete than the preceding, and is a close parallel to a medieval *tīrthankara* figure in *Figure B* the Mathurā museum (Figure B). Here on the base of the lion-throne, worn but intact, is the figure of a small bull which is the symbol for Rsabhanātha, the first of the twenty-four great saviors.

Standing at either side of the saint, and also somewhat broken, are two *yaksas* with their fly-whisks. Hovering above them and touching the ringed halo are the broken figures of two *gandhārvas*, or heavenly musicians, holding musical instruments or garlands. Originally a half-umbrella projected from the background above the saint's head, but this was broken away with the rest of the missing top area. Faintly visible, rising vertically from the top of the saint's head, is a shaft which originally supported the umbrella. The upper half of the slightly elliptical head is covered by numerous small nubs of curled hair common to both *tīrthankara* and Buddha images. The ears are elongated and touch the shoulders and, faintly visible in the center of the chest, is the *śrīvatsa* jewel.[13] The lion-throne again displays the two lions in threatening attitudes, as well as a figure in each of the recessed corners. The triangular drape and tassel again fall from the center of the throne, and are here much more elaborate in design than those of the previous example.

---

silenced, unable to refute him. His sermon is therefore the 'lion's roar' (*simhanāda*); for when the lion's voice is heard in the wilderness all other animals fall silent, fearing his approach."—*Ibid.*, p. 169.

12. For images of *tīrthankaras* and Buddhas from Mathurā see Coomaraswamy, *History of Indian and Indonesian Art*, figs. 84, 85, 86, 87; Coomaraswamy, "Origin of the Buddha Figure," figs. 39, 52, 64.

13. Compare this image's face with that of the standing figure of Rsabhanātha in Zimmer, *Art of Indian Asia*, II, Plate 389.

In fact, this elaborateness and softening of the form, especially apparent in the carving of the lions and of the saint's legs, point to a later and more sophisticated date of execution. This Jain image of the first *tīrthankara*, Rsabhanātha, must date from about the eleventh or twelfth century and come from Rājputāna or Mathurā.

The next two Jain sculptures in the Ringling Museum come from western India and are carved from a pure white marble which is associated with the temple complex at Mt. Ābū. One is an ornate pillar or door jamb fragment (Plate 9) and the other (Plate 7) is a rather worn and small image of the goddess Shrī-Lakshmī.

Plates 7 & 9

The possibility that the carved pillar was at one time a part of a temple shrine or cell becomes especially evident when it is compared with the door frame shown in the interior photo (Figure C) of the Rsabhanātha Temple at Mt. Ābū.[14] There at the bottom, on either side of the door, is seen, as in the museum's example, a standing male deity closed in by an elaborately carved niche. Above this niche are four smaller ones, each containing a seated deity complete with two female attendants. Since the museum's piece is broken at the top, only two and a half of the upper niches remain.

Figure C

Running vertically up the jamb at the left side of the plate is a wave or vine pattern, which as a symbolic motif on the doorway signifies the mystical anointment that occurs where the image and the worshipper "cross" the threshold.[15] The deity at the bottom of the pillar stands in a *tribhanga* (the three bends) position, wearing a crown and holding attributes; at his feet stands an animal which is undoubtedly his vehicle (*vāhana*). Comparison of this standing figure unit with those which are shown on the face of the columns in the foreground of Figure C shows a striking similarity between them. On the columns the figures are contained within a framework which is exactly duplicated on the museum's piece. Note especially the distinctive comma-like design carved into the pointed crown of the niche and the similarity of the ringed columns flanking the main standing figure, topped as they are by a rectangular shape containing a diamond design. The standing female attendants are not to be found on the large columns in the temple,

14. Other examples of Jain door jambs may be seen in Kramrisch, *Art of India*, plates 133 and 134.
15. For a discussion of the symbolic meaning of the temple's doorway see Kramrisch, *The Hindu Temple*, II, 313-322.

11

but are in evidence on either side of the cell's door frame as they evolve from a group of figures on the walls. In the museum's piece the attending figures are broken, but to the deity's extreme right can be seen the remains of a leg poised outward toward the edge.

This direction in which the attending figures face indicates that the jamb was located to the right as one faces the cell. Conclusive evidence is found in the small female figures kneeling in a worshipful attitude at the top and on either side of the niche's ornate crown. They face reverently to the left, the direction of the cell and the image of the *tīrthankara*.

Hindu deities were accepted and used by Jains as representing an aspect of earthly *karma* and as beings of a lower spiritual order aspiring to the perfection of the *tīrthankaras*. So it is not strange to see them used quite profusely in Jain temple sculpture. The identity of the standing god on this piece is obscure, even though his hands hold a drum and a possible club. This would normally indicate that the image is that of the lord Śiva, but since the other attributes are missing and the animal vehicle (*vāhana*) at his feet is broken, the identity cannot be positive. It will suffice to say that he is a god and that he is performing the service of an attendant or doorkeeper (*dvārapāla*) in the old *yakṣa* tradition which has already been observed on the *tīrthankara* images.

Judging by the above mentioned similarities between the museum's piece and the work in the Rṣabhanātha temple at Mt. Ābū, which was consecrated in 1031,[16] it is suggested that the piece is a door jamb from a Jain temple in southwest Rājputāna and dates from the eleventh or twelfth centuries.

Plate 7   The museum's last Jain sculpture also comes from western India and is a small and worn white marble figure of the lotus goddess Shri-Lakshmī (Plate 7). She is the universal mother, wife of Vishnu and the life-bestowing, benevolent goddess of prosperity and good fortune. "She presides over the fertility and moisture of the soil and over the jewels and precious metals in the womb of the earth."[17] Seated in a lotus position, she is shown here with four arms. Her lower right hand rests on her right leg, palm out, in the traditional *varada-mudrā*, or bestowing gifts, while her lower left hand holds what appears to be a jug, another symbol of abundance.

16. See Zimmer, *Art of Indian Asia*, II, 416, notes to plates 390, 391.
17. Zimmer, *Art of Indian Asia*, I, 158.

From her two raised hands hang broken lotus stems whose blossoms are completely missing. On either side of the goddess' head a platform supports an elephant with upraised trunk sprinkling her with the life-giving fertilizing waters. This rite of anointment is known as *abhiseka*, and because of the presence of the elephants (*gajas*) we can identify this aspect of the deity as Gaja-Lakshmī.[18] Her head supports what was once an elaborately pointed crown of several layers, and her ear ornaments (obscured by shadow in the photograph) with heavy rounded ends hang almost to her shoulders. A necklace loops over her ample breasts and a pendant appears between them. The depth of the carving testifies to the fact that the work was most elaborate and detailed before it became so broken and worn away.

The throne is difficult to make out, but the broken detail of an elephant's head directly in its center is perceptible. To either side of the elephant's head is seen a series of small three-layered nubs, possibly the vague remains of a lotus throne, the usual symbol of the lotus goddess. On the extreme sides and at the knees of Lakshmī can barely be discerned seated figures in worshipful attitudes.

One might be tempted to identify the central figure as the river goddess Sarasvati whose "images are sometimes hardly distinguishable from those of Shri-Lakshmī,"[19] especially since the stylistic resemblance between this figure and that of a twelfth-century image of Sarasvati being saluted by the two architects of the Vimala Vasahī at Mt. Ābū (Figure D) is so remarkable. The chief differences between the two figures are that in the Mt. Ābū figure the goddess' left hand holds a palm-leaf manuscript, her right a stylized lotus blossom, and her right leg drops down from the throne. Other iconographic details, including the stiff, rigid style, are the same.

Figure D

A similar and more significant image of Lakshmī surmounts the door frame of a side chapel in the Neminātha temple at Mt. Ābū (Figure E).[20] Judging by the apparent scale of the photograph, the museum's figure and the image over the cell of the doorway

Figure E

---

18. See Zimmer, *Myths and Symbols in Indian Art and Civilization*, pp. 102-109, for a discussion of elephants and their symbolic relation to fertility.
19. *Ibid.*, pp. 109-110.
20. "In many mediaeval temples, specially of Orissa, this motif is often described as Gaja-Lakshmī, was carved in the center of the architrave over the doorway of the main structure, whatever might have been the cult affiliation of the shrines."—Banerjea, *Development of Hindu Iconography*, p. 375.

are comparable in size and iconography. Here is the pointed and layered crown, the lower right hand performing the *varada-mudrā*, the left supporting the jug; the two stylized lotus blossoms supported by the raised hands explain the broken stems held by the upright hands in the museum's image. Even the mysterious three-layered nubs come into focus and become recognizably clear, as do the pendant and necklace over the breast. Only the elephants above the goddess and on the throne are missing, or perhaps are hidden from view as were those in the museum's piece before the lotuses were broken away.

It can be concluded, then, that the museum's image is a Jain sculpture of the goddess Gaja-Lakshmī from southwestern Rājputāna and dates from the twelfth or thirteenth century.

By the seventh century Buddhism was waning in the land of its birth, but in the monasteries of Bihār and Bengal there lingered a variant form of Mahāyāna Buddhism. This Tāntric Buddhism, as it was called, came to an end in India in 1199 when Nālandā and the other great centers of Buddhist learning were destroyed by the iconoclastic Moslems who raged down the Ganges Valley. It is from this last era of Buddhist activity, known as the Pāla period (760-1142), that the Ringling Museum's next two works come.

Both works are Buddha figures in the famous seated pose of calling the earth to witness (*bhūmi-sparśa-mudrā*), and each has suffered mutilation, presumably at the hands of the Moslems. Defaced in every detail, but the more complete, is the green-gray piece displaying seven of the eight great events in the Buddha's life (Plate 10). The central and dominant figure is that of the Buddha seated upon a lotus pedestal supported by a high and simple throne. On the throne in Devanagari script is carved a *mantra*, which is frequently found on Buddhist images of this period.[21]

Plate 10

In front of this inscription and at the very base of the throne are two smaller Buddhas seated in the *bhūmi-sparśa-mudrā* pose of the large central image.

Directly behind the large central Buddha is a niche carved in a very low and stylized relief of circles and concave squares sur-

---

21. I am indebted to Professor W. Norman Brown of the University Pennsylvania for the following translation of this *mantra*.
*The states of being which arise from a basis—
Their basis the Tathāgata has told;
And their cessation—this the Great Monk tells.*

PLATES

Pl. 1.—"The Presentation of the Four Bowls." Buddhist, Gandhāra, c. III century. Gray schist, slightly convex, 8' x 17". Ringling Museum of Art, Sarasota.

Pl. 2.—"The *Bodhisattva* Maitreya." Buddhist, Gandhāra, c. III century. Gray schist, 9½" x 13", Ringling Museum of Art, Sarasota.

Pl. 3.—A vertical relief displaying two events from the life of the Buddha. Top, "The Buddha Converting the *Yaksha* Atvika(?)"; bottom, "The Buddha Accepting the Casteless Girl as a Nun(?)." Buddhist, Gandhāra, c. III century. Gray schist, 17" x 11", Ringling Museum of Art, Sarasota.

Pl. 4.—Figures in adoration, a fragment from a "First Sermon." Buddhist, Hoti-Mardan, Gandhāra, III-IV century, Gray schist, 11¼" x 11", Ringling Museum of Art, Sarasota.

Pl. 5.—"*Tīrthankara*. Jain, Mathurā, IV-V century. Red sandstone, 28" x 23", Ringling Museum of Art, Sarasota.

Pl. 6.—Fragment of a plinth. Buddhist, Malakand Pass, Gandhāra, c. III century. Gray schist, 5½" x 4½", Ringling Museum of Art, Sarasota.

Pl. 7.—Goddess Gaja-Lakshmī. Jain, southwest Rājputāna, XII-XIII century. White marble, 18" x 13½", Ringling Museum of Art, Sarasota.

Pl. 8.—"The *Tīrthankara* Rsabhanātha." Jain, Mathurā or central India, c. XI-XII century. Red sandstone, 42″ x 23″, Ringling Museum of Art, Sarasota.

Pl. 9.—Fragment of a temple door jamb. Jain, southwest Rājputāna, XI-XII century. White marble, 48¼" x 13", Ringling Museum of Art, Sarasota.

Pl. 10.—A Buddha of the events displaying the *bhūmi-sparśa-mudrā*. Buddhist, Bengal or Bihār, Pāla period, c. X century. Green chlorite, 19" x 11½", Ringling Museum of Art, Sarasota.

Pl. 11.—A Buddha in *bhūmi-sparśa-mudrā*. Buddhist, Bihār, Pāla period, c. X century. Black carboniferous shale, 15½" x 13", Ringling Museum of Art, Sarasota.

Pl. 12.—The Lord Bhairava. Hindu, southern Rājputāna, X-XI century. Red sandstone, 37¾" x 21", Ringling Museum of Art, Sarasota.

Pl. 12A.—
Side-view of
Plate 12.

Pl. 13.—A Śaivite group. Hindu, Rājputāna, c. XII century. Cream sandstone, 23¾" x 15¾", Ringling Museum of Art, Sarasota.

Pl. 14.—The Goddess Durgā. Hindu, Rājputāna, c. late XVIII century. Cream sandstone with some red pigment clinging to the goddess' right arms, 53½" x 16½", Ringling Museum of Art, Sarasota.

Pl. 15.—An architectural fragment with a niche containing a standing figure of Buddha subduing the maddened elephant (seen to the left at his feet). Buddhist, Pāla period, Bihār, c. X century. Black stone, 10¾" x 17", Ringling Museum of Art, Sarasota.

Pl. 16.—An architectural fragment with a niche containing a standing figure of Buddha. He displays the *varada-mudrā* to a small worshiping figure at his feet. Buddhist, Pāla period, Bihār, c. X century. Gray-green stone, 7½" x 15", Ringling Museum of Art, Sarasota.

Pl. 17.—A badly worn image of Śiva. Hindu, Rājputāna, c. XIII-XIV century. Marble, 20¼" x 9½", Ringling Museum of Art, Sarasota.

FIGURES

Fig. A.—"Shrine of the Wheel of the Law" (adoration of the Buddha who is symbolized by a wheel). Buddhist, Bhārhut, central India, c. II century B.C. Red sandstone, 18⅞″ x 20¾″, Freer Gallery of Art, Washington.

Fig. B.—"*Tīrthankara* Nemināthā." Jain, Mathurā, central India, medieval period. Red sandstone, h. 53½″. Photo courtesy the Archaeological Museum, Mathurā.

Fig. C.—Interior view of Vimala Shā's temple to Ṛsabhanātha at Mt. Ābū. Jain, Gujarāt, India, consecrated 1031. White marble. Photo after Zimmer, *The Art of Indian Asia.*

Fig. D.—The Goddess Sarasvatī saluted by the two architects who built the Vimala Vasahī temple. Mt. Ābū, Jain, south Rājputāna, XII century. White marble, 4½′ diameter. Photo after Kramrisch, *The Art of India*.

Fig. E.—Side chapel, Tejahpāla's temple to Neminātha at Mt. Ābū. Jain, southwest Rājputāna, 1232. White marble. Photo after Zimmer, *The Art of Indian Asia*.

Fig. F.—A Buddha (*Bodhisattva*) image displaying the eight miracles. Buddhist, Bengal, Pāla period, X-XI century. Black slate, h. 17¾″, Rijksmuseum voor Volkenkunde, Leiden.

Fig. G.—A couple of male *Dvārapālas* on the second small shrine at Chandravati. Hindu, Kotah, south central Rājputāna, VII-VIII century. After photo by D. H. Sahiar, *Marg* Magazine, XII (March, 1959), 40, Plate 3.

Fig. H.—A group of celestial figures from the upper tiers of the main temple in Rāmgarh. Hindu, Kotah, south central Rājputāna, early medieval. After photo by D. H. Sahiar in *Marg* Magazine, XII (March, 1959) 65, Plate 2.

Fig. I.—A sculptural group. Hindu, Bundelkhand?, central India, X-XII century. Cream sandstone, h. ? Photo courtesy Museum of Fine Arts, Boston.

Fig. J.—A Umā-Maheśvara group. Hindu, Pallū, Rājputāna, XI-XII century. h. 23" x 15½", Bikānēr Museum, India. Photo after Goetz, *The Art and Architecture of Bikaner State*.

Fig. X.—The Devāli of Mandala Rimanalota. Hindu, Savunda, Bikānēr, 1505. Bikānēr Museum, India. Photo after Goetz, *The Art and Architecture of Bikaner State*.

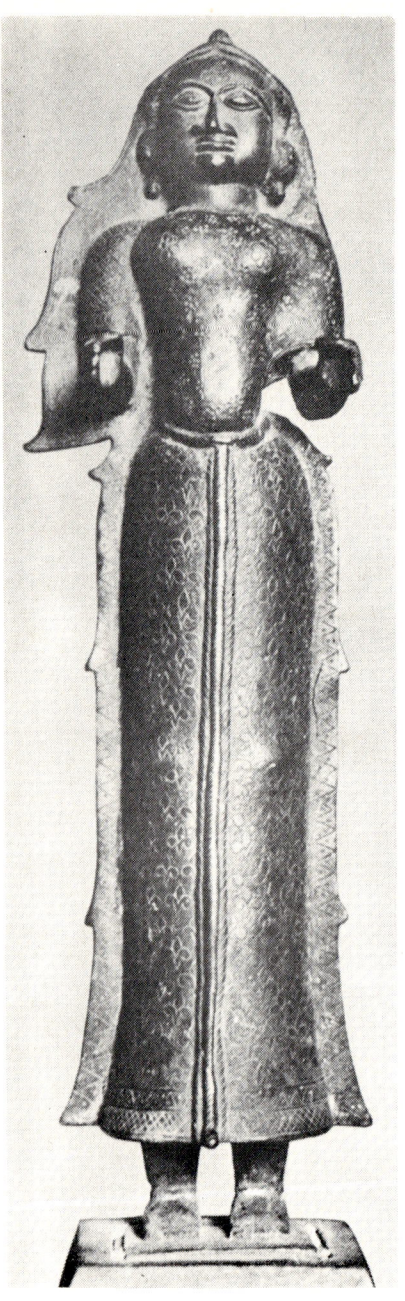 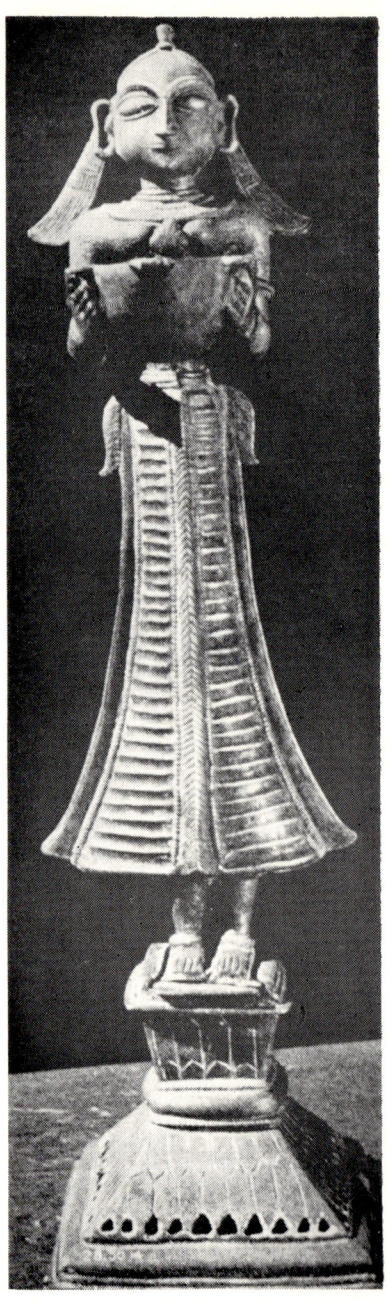

Fig. L.—A Dīpa-Lakshmī (lampbearer) figure. Hindu, Gujarāt, late XVII century. Brass, h. 14½". Courtesy of Baroda Museum, India.

Fig. M.—A Dīpa-Lakshmī (lampbearer) figure. Hindu, Gujarāt, c. XVIII century. Brass, Prince of Wales Museum, Bombay, India. Photo after Kramrisch, *The Art of India*.

mounted above by a halo of dots and flames. At the zenith of the halo are three stylized leaves representing the Bo-tree under which the enlightenment occurred. Around the edge of the background slab, circling the Buddha, are seven units in relief containing events from his life. Supported by lotus pedestals and ringed by dot patterns, these units are small duplicates of the larger sculptural unit. The only exception is the event at the top which shows the death, or *parinirvāna*, of the Buddha. The small seated figure at the feet of the recumbent Buddha is his chief disciple, Ānanda. On either side of this event are clouds containing a pair of celestial hands. The hands to the right hold cymbals and the ones to the left beat a drum. The cymbals and the drum represent universal rhythm (the pulse of creation) and sound (the vehicle of speech and the conveyor of revelation). These two symbols may be interpreted to stand for the divine truth of the law (*dharmā*) personified by the Buddha.

The work is similar to the Pāla image of the same subject in the Rijksmuseum voor Volkenkunde, Leiden (Figure F). The chief iconographic difference is that the Leiden image shows the Buddha with a crown and jewels, or as a *bodhisattva*, while the Ringling Museum's figure is a true Buddha in monastic garb. The Ringling figure is decorated only by the nubbed pattern of shorn hair on his head and a *ushnīsha*, or protubcrance, at the top of the skull; his simple throne contrasts vividly with the lion-throne at the base of the Leiden image.

Figure F

The eight events described on the Leiden image, clockwise from the lower left, are:
(1) The nativity,
(2) the first sermon,
(3) the descent from the Trayastrimśa heaven,
(4) the death or *parinirvāna*,
(5) the taming of the maddened elephant,
(6) the miracle of Śrāvastī,
(7) the monkey's offering, and
(8) the central and dominant scene of the enlightenment. On either side of the *parinirvāna*, at the top, are seated two large *dhyāni* Buddhas.

Other than the elaborate headdress, the most important difference between the Ringling Museum's work and the Leiden image is the arrangement and number of the events surrounding the main figure. The nativity is completely missing from the Ringling Museum's work, and in its place is a duplicate scene of the monkey's offering. This means that the piece displays only seven of the eight great events. They are, clockwise from the lower left:

(1) the monkey's offering (note the monkey sculptured in low relief just beneath the seated Buddha);

(2) the descent from the Trayastrimśa heaven (missing here, but present in Figure F, is the figure of Indra holding an umbrella over the Buddha's head);

(3) the preaching of the first sermon in the deer park at Benares (on the base of the lotus pedestal is the wheel symbol [*cakra*] for the law [*dharma*] flanked by the seated figures of two deer)—the Buddha above holds his hands in the *dharmā-cakra-mudrā*;

(4) the *parinirvāna*, or the great demise;

(5) the miracle of Śrāvastī (note the seated figure seated at the base of the lotus pedestal);

(6) the taming of the maddened elephant (the elephant, as seen in Plate 15, is the very small figure at the Buddha's feet);

(7) a duplicate scene of the monkey's offering; and

(8) the enlightenment (represented by the large central Buddha figure in the *bhūmi-sparśa-mudrā*).

The two small Buddha figures at the base of the work might also symbolize the miracle of Śrāvastī, but they could more likely represent, along with the large central figure, the manifestation of *trikāya*, or the three bodies of the Buddha.[22] The use of only seven events is hard to explain, especially with the nativity missing; and the mystery is disturbing. One possible explanation might be, as indeed the style suggests, that the main image of the Buddha was carved by one sculptor, while the smaller events were executed by another, a less competent craftsman. The sculptor of the events then may have miscopied them from another image. This, of course, is pure speculation.

Plate 11   The museum's second Pāla image of the Buddha (Plate 11) is carved from a hard black stone typical of works coming from

22. "One of the concepts of Mahāyāna Buddhism that finds its inevitable reflexion in the iconography of that art is the *trikāya*, or Three Bodies of Buddha. This triune division of the Buddha nature is, in a philosophical sense, analogous to the Christian trinity. In this triune nature we have the *dharmakāya* or 'Law Body' . . . the *sambhogakāya* or 'Body of Bliss' . . . and the third body, the *nirmānakāya* or 'Noumenal Body.'" A footnote to this sentence further points out that "the crowned and bejewelled Buddhas of Pāla-Sena times have been interpreted as representations of the body of bliss." —Rowland, *Art and Architecture of India*, pp. 32-33, 258, n. 12.

Nālandā.[23] The obdurate quality of the stone accounts for the fact that the compact body was not more extensively damaged when the background slab was broken away. All that remains of the background is a small fragment above the image's right shoulder which displays a portion of a nimbus or halo. The face of the image, originally broken away, was recarved by an inept craftsman at a later date.

The Buddha is again seen in the pose of *bhūmi-sparśa-mudrā* and his right hand, with the forefinger missing, is stretched out and touching the lotus pedestal. This carving is from a more competent hand than was evidenced in the previous Pāla image. Here is a refinement of form and a sensitiveness for realism in the detailing that was less marked in the first Pāla Buddha. Indeed it is this very quality which marks the piece as distinctively Pāla.

Commenting on the Pāla style, Dr. B. Rowland makes the following observations. "Characteristic of the sculpture of the Pāla and Sena periods are the numerous examples of images carved in hard, black stone found at Nālandā and many other sites in [Bihār and] Bengal. All of them are characterized by great finesse and precision of execution. Many of these icons give the impression of being stone imitations of metal-work, and in almost every case the sense of plastic conception is lost under the intricacy of surface detail." And, "The actual style of carving is a kind of desiccated perpetuation of the Gupta school of the fifth and sixth centuries; in it one is much more conscious of the precise and sharp definition of the detail of jewelled ornaments than of the plastic significance of the bodily form that seems to exist as a framework for these attributes."[24]

Recognizing these facts and comparing the two images with the work mentioned, it would seem that the first green-gray image, displaying events from the Buddha's life and inscribed with a *mantra*, is a Pāla Buddha from Bengal or Bihār and dates from the tenth century. The second Buddha is also a tenth century Pāla work carved in Bihār by a more skillful sculptor.

One of the terrifying aspects of Śiva is the featured image of the next work (Plate 12). He is carved on the face of a rectangular block of pink sandstone, which at one time possibly formed part of a vertical buttress, from a Śaivite temple. The figure stands be-

Plate 12

23. Coomaraswamy, *Indian and Indonesian Art,* p. 113.
24. *Art and Architecture of India,* p. 144.

tween two ringed columns which in turn are flanked high on either side by a vertical relief of mythical animals. Below these reliefs and at the feet of the image run two horizontal mouldings carved across the front, behind the figure, and around the right corner of the block. These mouldings, it can be assumed, ran throughout the building as a unifying architectural device.

Plate 12A On the side of this block (Plate 12A) to the viewer's left and above the center moulding is carved a flat elaborate column featuring the traditional Hindu pot-foliage capital (*pūrnakalaśa*).[25] Directly beneath this column and under the moulding kneels a four-armed figure of a *gana*, one of the departed souls who constitute Śiva's celestial army.[26] With two arms he supports the moulding and in turn the column above, while his lower right hand holds a sword, and his left a shield. He wears a loincloth, bracelets, and a small necklace. The remainder of the vertical surface to the left is set back from the plane of the column-*gana* unit and is composed of a shallow and simply carved vine or wave motif, while below the moulding is displayed a diamond-shaped flower with four petals.

On the front of the block the animal reliefs to either side of the columns flanking the standing deity can be read from top to bottom as a crocodile or sea monster (*makara*), a rampant lion (*śārdūla*), and an elephant's head. The most important image of this trio is the lion. He represents the eternal words of knowledge, and elsewhere in Indian art supports by his regal and earth-penetrating roar the thrones of the world saviors (the Buddhas and *tīrthankaras*). Here the *śārdūla* dances upon the elephant's head of ignorance, while, above, the *makara*, symbolic of the powers of waters, fearful and benign, blesses the triumph of knowledge over ignorance by anointing the scene with life-giving fluid.[27]

The major figure, Bhairava, has four arms and stands with his weight shifted slightly to his left leg. The god seems to be standing upon an object or animal of some kind, but because of its broken and worn condition its identity is impossible to ascertain. His upper right hand holds high the small "hour-glass" drum (*damaru*), while his lower right arm extends rigidly down with its hand turned

25. For the historical and architectural significance of this capital design see Fergusson, *Indian and Far Eastern Architecture*, I, 317-318.
26. These hosts are led by the elephant-headed son of Śiva (See Plate 13).
27. For a discussion of the symbolic meanings of the *śārdūla* and the *makara* see Kramrisch, *Hindu Temple*, II, 322-331.

in and finger extended to support an obscure object which might be either a throwing disc (*cakra*) or a bowl made from a skull (*bhiksāpātra*). A staff or club (*khatvānga*) displaying a small round skull and topped by a trident (*triśūla*) is held aloft by the upper left hand, while the deity's lower left hand holds a lotus blossom to his chest. This blossom symbolizes the lingam, or phallus, the major symbol of the lord Śiva, and the lotus itself is the symbol *par excellence* of eternal generation. On the lord's wrists, upper arms, and ankles are simple bracelets, and across his chest hang several necklaces. He supports from his waist a girdle which shows in high relief between his legs. A garland of human skulls (*asthibūshana*) drops from the shoulders, twines through his arms, and loops across his legs just below the knees. The head, whose features have mostly been worn away, is surmounted by a high crown of matted hair (*jata-makuta*), and two ear ornaments hang down and rest on the god's shoulders.

Perhaps the most distinguishing feature of this image is its large head, whose size can be explained, possibly, by the iconographic canon which requires the images of Śiva in his terrific aspects to "have bulging eyes, inflated cheeks, tusks, etc."[28] Here it would seem that not just the cheeks but the whole head has been "inflated" to enhance its demonic aspect. And even though the features of the face are lacking, two strong cavities or indentions can be discerned at the extreme corners of the mouth. These could possibly indicate the past presence of a grimace or the prescribed tusks or fangs. The shadowy forms of the eyes also suggest a bulging that would further confirm the identity of Bhairava.[29]

There can be little doubt that the figure comes from the face of a temple, and this origin is even further suggested by small fragments of plaster, flaked in layers, still clinging to the carved recesses deep in the stone. The practice of washing whole temples with a gesso-like plaster was widespread, and "the calm radiance

28. *Ibid.*, p. 330, n. 96.

29. For some descriptions of deities in paintings allied to music see Gangoly, Rāgas & Rāginīs, pp. 106-107, 111, 113. Professor Gangoly translates (p. 111) from the RAGA-MALA text by Mesakarna (1509) a description of Bhairava which is most appropriate to our image: "White in complexion, clad in white, carrying the crescent and the horn, and wearing a garland, Bhairava is born from the mouth of Śiva, and carries the poison on his neck and his eyes are red. He (also) carries the trident, the skull, and the lotus, and wears jewelled pendants on his two ears and matted locks. This (melody) is sung by the gods in the morning in Autumn."

of the white temples is extolled in inscriptions."³⁰ The temple was a "world-mountain" and the attribute of a white, shimmering snow-like quality was in keeping with the abode of the gods (*himālaya*, the abode of snow).

The style of the work, a medieval piece, is quite different from the great masterwork found on the temples of Khajurāho. But Dr. Kramrisch in discussing some of the major characteristics of those images describes a condition which is parallelled here: "Framed however in their niches, each a small shrine, pillared and having frequently a superstructure and roof of their own, the major divinities are sheltered, each niche being a paradoxical massive-door in which is beheld an aspect of the divinity of the temple."³¹ She further states in a note to this paragraph that "In Khajurāho, however, the pillared niche with its canopy is a balcony-like projection from its buttresses. That is the rule also in Rājputāna, Gujarāt, etc."³²

A closer parallel in style, however, occurs in the early medieval sculpture of the state of Kotah in southeastern Rājputāna. The images at Chandravati (Figure G) display the large head which is seen in the museum's image, and at Rāmgarh the figures on the upper tiers of the main temple (Figure H) illustrate a stage in "the transition of the Khajurāho style to the more primitive but vital chisel in the interior of Rājasthan."³³ This identification of style very well describes the museum's image of Bhairava.

Considering all the aspects above, it is probable that the museum's figure is a temple sculpture of Bhairava, one of the terrific forms of Śiva, from southern Rājputāna, and dates from the tenth or the eleventh century.

A sculptural fragment displaying Śaivite images is the next work from central India (Plate 13). Carved from buff sandstone this small medieval masterpiece shows four figures, three standing and one kneeling. The two standing images to the left are the "mind born" children of the lord Śiva and his consort Pārvatī. The third is probably an attending *yaksa*, while the kneeling figure is most likely that of a female donor.

30. Kramrisch, *Hindu Temple*, I, 123.
31. *Ibid.*, II, 318.
32. *Ibid.*, n. 49.
33. D. S., "Medieval Sculpture, ※12: Ramgarh," *Marg* Magazine, XIII, (March, 1959), 65.

The gods feared the offspring of such a terrible union as that of Śiva and Pārvatī and requested of Śiva that he have no children. This he agreed to without informing Pārvatī, and she, when told, was so enraged that she cursed the wives of the other gods to a similar state. Therefore all the children of the gods are referred to as being "mind born."

The figure to the extreme left, with an elephant's head, is that of Gaṇeśa who, according to one legend was created out of clay by Pārvatī.[34] Śiva, not knowing the boy's identity, later beheaded him, and as the head was severed from Gaṇeśa's body, it shot up into the sky and disappeared. Since it could not be recovered, Śiva decapitated a baby elephant who was nearby and placed its head upon the body of Gaṇeśa.[35]

Gaṇeśa as the god of prudence and sagacity is seen in Indian banks, shops, and libraries. Being the remover of obstacles, he is propitiated before any undertaking, attached to the tops of letters, and always saluted at the beginning of a book.

Here he wears a girdle, necklace, bracelets, head jewels, and short pants, with a garland circling below his knees. The attribute in his right hand is missing, but it was probably one of his tusks which was broken off in a mythical battle.

Gaṇeśa's vehicle (*vāhana*), a rat, is not shown here, but next to him is his brother, the god of war Kārttikeya, or Skanda, astride his *vāhana*, a peacock.

The *asura* (demon) Tāraka through penitence gained a boon from Brahmā which gave him not only power over the three worlds, but over the gods as well. This boon granted him exemption from death at the hand of all except the offspring of the celibate Śiva. After suffering many indignities under the demon, the gods at last pleaded with Śiva to produce such progeny. Thus it was that Kārttikeya was created, the first son of Śiva, and seven days later the scourge of the gods was dead.[36]

One legend tells of Kārttikeya assuming six heads at birth in order to be nursed by the Pleiades, but here we see him with only three heads (the one on his left shoulder is obscured). He stands

---

34. "Gaṇeśa—Lord (*īśa*) of the hosts (*gaṇa*)." He is also known as "Vighneśvara—Lord (*īśvara*) of obstacles (*vighna*)."—Zimmer, *Art of Indian Asia*, I, 46.
35. Thomas, *Epics, Myths and Legends of India*, pp. 24-25.
36. Ibid., pp. 26-27.

in a *tribhanga* pose and holds in his left hand a club-like weapon, or a *cauri*. Under his right arm he holds a cock, another of his symbols, whose head has been broken away and only the body and tail feathers remain. A garland circles his body, and his other ornaments include a necklace, a girdle, and heavy earrings. His heads are dressed by high spiraling crowns or coiffures, while his lower body is clothed only in short pants.

The third standing figure is possibly a *yaksha*, and he holds what appears as a club rather than the usual *cauri*, or fly-whisk. He, too, stands in the *tribhanga* pose which the sculptor utilized as a device to unify the three vertical figures and give action to the unit. In respect to ornaments and dress, he duplicates those of the Kārttikeya figure and his jaws also display a slight broadening which is "a characteristic later very common to the decadent phase of medieval sculpture."[37]

On the extreme right of the thick base (common to all the figures) is a broken foot wearing an anklet. This is all that remains of the large standing image which was the main subject of the work. Because of the presence of the "children" of Śiva and Pārvatī, it is fairly certain that the large figure was that of either their mother or their father. As the base steps back with each of the standing figures, it forms a plane of depth which evolved upward into a niche or gateway (*torna*) to contain the large missing image. This, when the work was unbroken, joined the quartet with another group of attending figures on the right.

Figure I

A sculptural fragment similar to this one is found in the Museum of Fine Arts at Boston. It is thought to come from Bundelkhand and dates in the period from the tenth to the twelfth century (Figure I). It, too, displays one kneeling and three standing figures, and it formed the left side of a *torna* containing a large image. The style of the carving, however, retains a hint of the rounded and classical mode, which indicates that the Ringling Museum's piece was executed later.

Figure J

The Umā-Maheśvara Group from Pallū (Figure J), now in the Bīkānēr Museum, dates from the eleventh or twelfth century and stylistically represents a closer parallel to the Ringling Museum work. This is especially noticeable in the small three-headed figure standing to the extreme left, which is identified by Dr. Goetz as

---

37. Goetz, *Art and Architecture of Bikaner State*, p. 87.

Brahmā but which is more likely that of Kārttikeya. Note particularly the small figure's *tribhanga* pose, the squared jaw, and the general sculptural style of the whole piece. Since the Ringling Museum's work is stylistically closer to this piece, it is suggested that this Śaivite fragment comes from Rājputāna and dates from the twelfth century.

The "Great Mother" is not only the most ancient of deities, but as Dr. Goetz has observed, her cult is the oldest still existing in Rājputāna.[38] It is therefore appropriate that the last work from Rājputāna is a late image of the goddess Durgā (Plate 14). This work displays scarcely a trace of the great sculptural idiom of the medieval period, being closer in spirit to folk sculpture, but its primitive and abstracted style is attractive to the contemporary eye.

Plate 14

Durgā, known as Kālī and Cāmundā in southern India, was brought into being by the combined energies of the gods to aid them in their battles against the *asuras*, or demons.[39] As the fierce and triumphant avenger of the gods, she here appears somewhat benign, displaying only four arms rather than the seventeen bestowed upon her by the gods at her mythical creation.

If this aspect of the goddess were either Kālī or Cāmundā, the figure would appear much more hideous, with an emaciated body, hollow cheeks, bulging eyes, and lolling tongue. But here the goddess stands at ease with just the slightest suggestion of the *tribhanga* pose. She displays four braceleted arms, and two surprisingly small discs high on her chest indicate her breasts. A necklace loops between the breasts, and another circles her throat; a crown, similar to many found in late Mogul and Rājput paintings, is seen on her large head. Anklets, ear ornaments, a girdle, a bodice, and long pants complete her costume.

On the goddess' forehead there is a horizontal mark and below it, between her eyes, is a *ūrnā*; on each cheek there is a dot. On each of her biceps is indicated a flower blossom which most likely represents a tatoo, since a similar flower can be seen on the right hand which holds a trident. The other right hand holds a sword, and in the two left hands she carries a snake and a bowl for blood or lifegiving nectar. Standing behind her at her feet is her *vāhana*, a primitively carved dog-like lion.

38. *Ibid.*, p. 30.
39. "Durgā, she who is difficult (*dur*) to go against (*ga*)."—Zimmer, *Art of Indian Asia*, I, 90.

Figure K

Figure L

Figure M

This less sophisticated piece is closely related to the productions of folk art, and if it is compared with some works from Rājputāna and Gujarāt, some interesting similarities will be seen.

Figure K shows a Devālī, or memorial stone, for one of the Bikānēr *rājās*. This piece dates from the early sixteenth century and shows the *rājā* on horseback, while before him stand three of his queens, or *rānīs*, who committed *satī* at his death. Although this piece is quite worn, there is a strong resemblance between these stiff images and the Durgā figure. The oversize heads, the large ear ornaments, and the long straight legs with high anklets suggest the forms which later evolve in the museum's work. Similar memorial slabs are still being executed today in Rājputāna and follow the old and repetitive formulae.[40]

A little later in date and more western in provenance are two brass figures of Dīpa Lakshmī lampbearers from Gujarāt (Figures L and M). The older one (Figure L) is in the Baroda Museum and dates from the late seventeenth century. It shows a family likeness both to the *satī* figures on the stele and to the image of Durgā. Notice the shape of the head, especially the nose and mouth areas, the small high breasts, and the exceedingly long straight legs, skirt, and girdle. In the second lampbearer figure (Figure M) occur the same general characteristics, which possess, however, a more overt decorativeness. Notice especially the ears which duplicate those of the Durgā figure.

It must be remembered that these bronzes are much smaller than the stone image and were cast by the cire-perdue method which permits and encourages more ornamentation than does the more obdurate stone. But these examples, along with the stele figures, show the persistence of an image type in the folk mode of west central India which is over a thousand years old, and it is from this image that our Durgā figure emanates.

Because of the strong resemblance between the Ringling Museum's work and the *satī* figures on the stele and the bronzes from western Gujarāt, it may be surmised that the image of Durgā is not too modern, and an approximate date of the late eighteenth century and a provenance of Rājputāna are suggested.

---

40. Goetz, *Art and Architecture of Bikaner State*, p. 96.

CHRONOLOGICAL TABLE

	INDIA	OTHER
3,500 B.C.	Indus valley civilization, c. 2,500-1,500 B.C.	Mesopotamiam cities, c. 3,500-1,000 B.C. Solomon, 10th century B.C.
1,500 B.C.	Āryan invasion of India. Destruction of the Indus valley civilization. Vedic period, c. 1,500-800 B.C.	Achaemenid Persian Empire, 550-330 B.C.
500 B.C.	Buddha, c. 563-483 B.C. Mahāvīra, d. c. 468 B.C.	Plato, 427?-347 B.C.
300 B.C.	Alexander the Great crossed the Indus river, 326 B.C. Chandragupta Maurya, c. 321-297 B.C. Aśoka, c. 273-232 B.C. Bhārhut, Sānchī, 3rd cent. B.C.–1st cent. of Christ. era	Seleucid Persian Empire, 305-64 B.C.
100 B.C.	Early Mathurā. Early Ajantā caves. Hīnayāna Buddhism.	
0	Beginnings of Gandhāran Art. Amarāvatī.	Christ.
100	Mahāyāna Buddhism. Kanishka, Kusāna King, c. 120?-162.	Trajan, Roman Emperor, 98-117. Palmyra, 105.
300	Chandragupta I, 320-c. 335. Gupta Art, 4th-7th cents. White Huns invade India, c. 460. Gandāhra laid waste.	Rome falls, 476.
500	Medieval Indian Art, c. 550-1550.	Mohammed, 570?-632.

	Māmallapuram, early 7th cent.	
	Arab conquest of Sind, c. 712.	
	Pāla Dynasty of Bengal founded by Gopāla, c. 750	Charlemagne, 742-814.
1000	Khajurāho.	
	Konārak.	
	Moslem conquest of northern India, 1192-96.	
	Nālandā destroyed, 1199.	
	End of Buddhism in India.	Aquinas, 1225-1274.
1500	Moghul Period, 1526-1857.	First Portuguese and English in India.
	Akbar, 1556-1605.	
	Rājput dynasties, 1500-1850.	
	Gandhi, 1869-1948.	Darwin, 1809-1882.
1947	Indian independence.	

BIBLIOGRAPHY

Archer, W. G. *The Vertical Man*. London: George Allen & Unwin, Ltd., 1947.
Ashton, Sir L. (ed.) *The Art of India and Pakistan: The Commemorative Catalogue of the Exhibition Held at the Royal Academy of Art, London, 1947-8*. New York: Coward-McCann, Inc., n.d.
Banerjea, J. *The Development of Hindu Iconography (2nd ed.)*. Calcutta: University of Calcutta, 1956.
Basham, A. L. *The Wonder That Was India*. London: Macmillan & Co., 1954.
Burnier, Raymond. *Hindu Medieval Sculpture*. Paris: La Palme, 1950.
Coomaraswamy, Ananda K. "A Buddhist Sculpture," *Museum of Fine Arts Bulletin* (Boston), XXII (1924), 30.
―――. *History of Indian and Indonesian Art*. London: Edw. Goldston, 1927.
―――. "Sculptures from Mathurā," *Museum of Fine Arts Bulletin* (Boston) Vol. XXV, No. 150 (1927), 50.
―――. "The Origin of the Buddha Figure," *The Art Bulletin*, IX (1927), 287-329.
―――. *The Transformation of Nature in Art*, Cambridge (Mass.): Harvard University Press, 1935.
―――. *The Dance of Shiva (rev. ed.)*. New York: The Noonday Press, 1957.
―――. *Hinduism and Buddhism*. New York: Philosophical Library, n.d.
D. S. "Medieval Sculpture, #12: Ramgarh," *Marg* Magazine (Bombay), XII, (March, 1959), 64-66.
Fergusson, James. *The History of Indian and Far Eastern Architecture*. 2 vols. New York: Dodd, Mead and Co., 1899.
Foucher, A. *L'Art Greco-Bouddhique du Gandhāra*. 2 vols. Paris: École Française d'Éxtrême Orient, 1905-18.
Gangoly, O. G. *Rāgas and Rāginīs (2nd ed.)*. Bombay: Nalanda Publications, 1948.
Goetz, Hermann. *The Art and Architecture of Bīkānēr State*. Oxford: Bruno Cassirer, 1950.
―――. *India, Five Thousand Years of Indian Art*. New York: McGraw Hill Book Co., 1958.
Grousset, René. *Civilizations of the East. vol. 2: India*. New York: 1931.
Humphreys, Christmas. *Buddhism*. Harmondsworth: Penguin Books, 1952.
Ingholt, Harald. *Gandhāran Art in Pakistan*. New York: Pantheon Books, 1957.
Kramrisch, Stella. *The Hindu Temple*. 2 vols. Calcutta: University of Calcutta, 1946.
―――. *The Art of India*. New York: Phaidon Press, 1954.
Lommel, Andreas. *Indische Kunst*. Munich: Staatliches Museum für Völkerkunde, 1958.
Marshall, Sir John. *The Buddhist Art of Gandhāra*. Cambridge: Cambridge University Press, 1960.
―――. *A Guide to Taxila*. Cambridge: Cambridge University Press, 1960.
Piggott, Stuart. *Prehistoric India to 1000 B.C.* (2nd ed.). Harmondsworth: Penguin Books, 1950.

Rowland, Benjamin. "A Revised Chronology of Gandhāra Sculpture." *The Art Bulletin*, XVIII (1936), 387-400.
———. *The Art and Architecture of India*. Baltimore: Penguin Books, 1953.
———. *Gandhāra Sculpture from Pakistan Museums*. New York: The Asia Society, 1960.
Saunders, E. Dale. *Mudrā*. New York: Pantheon Books, 1960.
Smith, Vincent. *The Oxford History of India* (3rd ed.). London: Oxford University Press, 1958.
Thomas, P. *Epics, Myths and Legends of India* (2nd ed.). Bombay: Taraporevala Sons & Co., n. d.
Wheeler, Sir Mortimer. *Rome Beyond the Imperial Frontiers*. Harmondsworth: Penguin Books, 1955.
———. *Early India and Pakistan*. London: Thames & Hudson, 1959.
Zimmer, Heinrich. *Myths and Symbols in Indian Art and Civilization*. New York: Pantheon Books, 1946.
———. *Philosophies of India*. New York: Pantheon Books, 1951.
———. *The Art of Indian Asia*. 2 vols. New York: Pantheon Books, 1955.

UNIVERSITY OF FLORIDA MONOGRAPHS

Humanities

No. 1 (Spring 1959): *The Uncollected Letters of James Gates Percival*
Edited by Harry R. Warfel

No. 2 (Fall, 1959): *Leigh Hunt's Autobiography The Earliest Sketches*
Edited by Stephen F. Fogle

No. 3 (Winter 1960): *Pause Patterns in Elizabethan and Jacobean Drama*
By Ants Oras

No. 4 (Spring 1960): *Rhetoric and American Poetry of the Early National Period*
By Gordon E. Bigelow

No. 5 (Fall 1960): *The Background of*
The Princess Casamassima
By W. H. Tilley

No. 6 (Winter 1961): Indian Sculpture in the John and Mable Ringling Museum of Art
By Roy C. Craven, Jr.